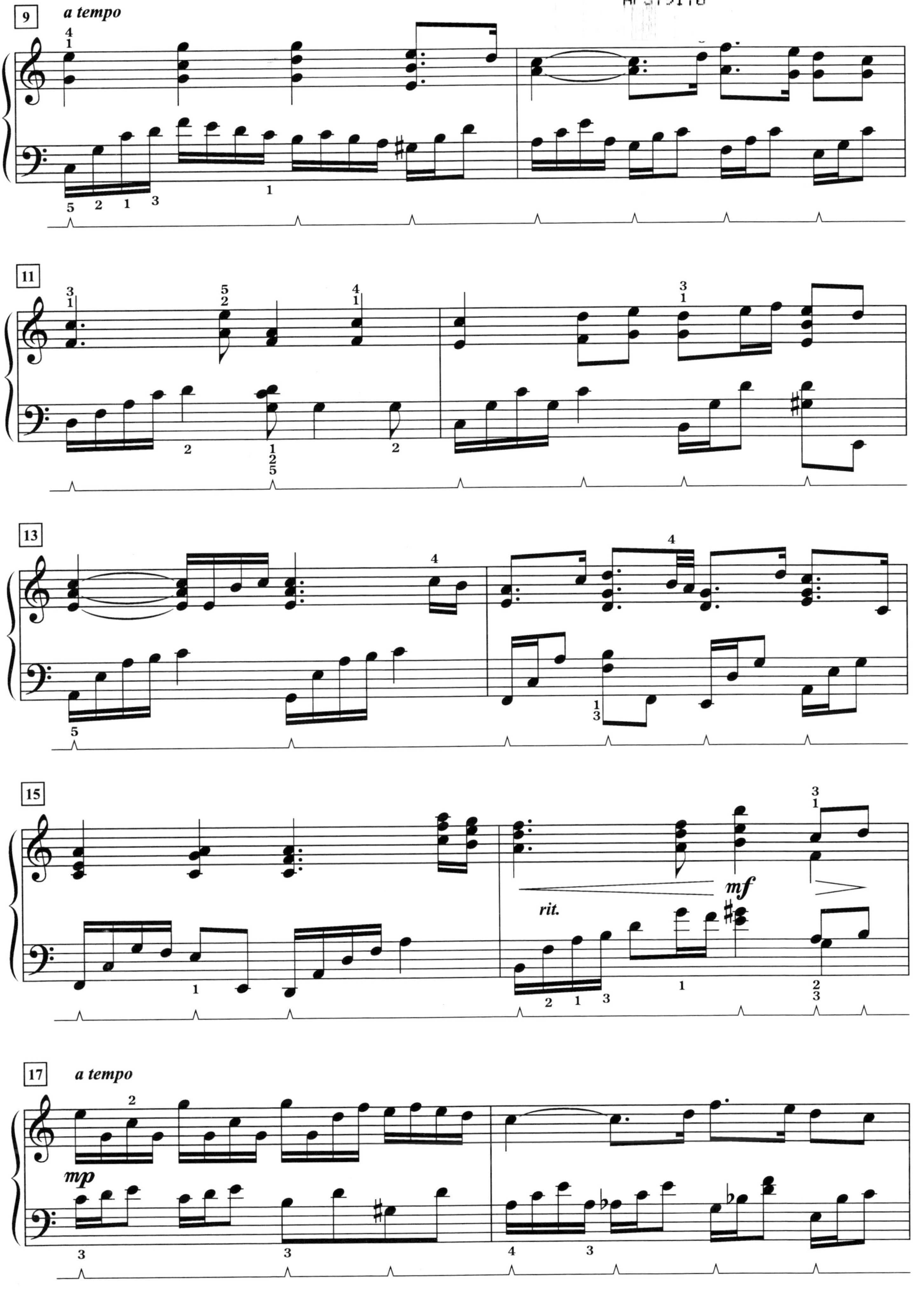
9
a tempo
11
13
15
rit.
mf
17
a tempo
mp

19
21
molto rit. p
24
a tempo
mp
27
29

5
31
mf
33
a tempo
35
4 1
4 2 1
f
molto rit.
3
38
4 2 1
4
mp
2 1
3
41
4
molto rit.
p
8va

The Heart of Worship

Come, let us bow down in worship, let us kneel before the Lord our Maker;
for he is our God and we are the people of his pasture, the flock under his care.
—Psalm 95:6–7 (NIV)

Words and Music by Matt Redman
Arr. Carol Tornquist

13
16
a tempo
poco rit.
19
22
25
mf

28
31
a tempo
poco rit.
f
34
3
3
37
3
40
Broadly
3
rit.

9
43
46
3
3
a tempo
49
mf
poco rit.
52
3
2
55
3
3
molto rit.
mp

(Approx. Performance Time – 2:00)

You're Worthy of My Praise

Let them praise the name of the Lord, for his name alone is exalted;
his splendor is above the earth and the heavens.

—Psalm 148:13 (NIV)

Words and Music by David Ruis
Arr. Carol Tornquist

13
16
19
rit.
4
2
1
a tempo
mf
22
25

28
a tempo
rit.
f
3

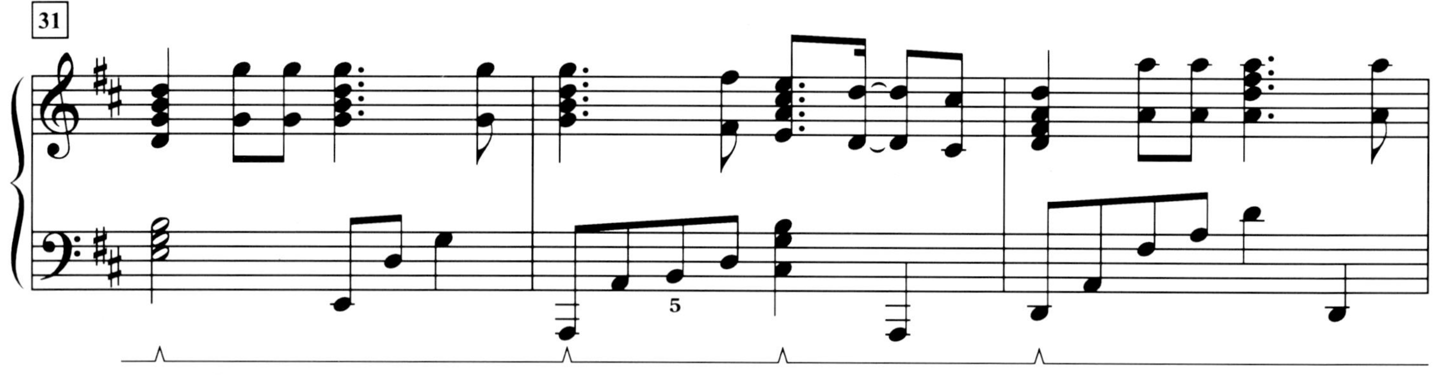

31
5

34

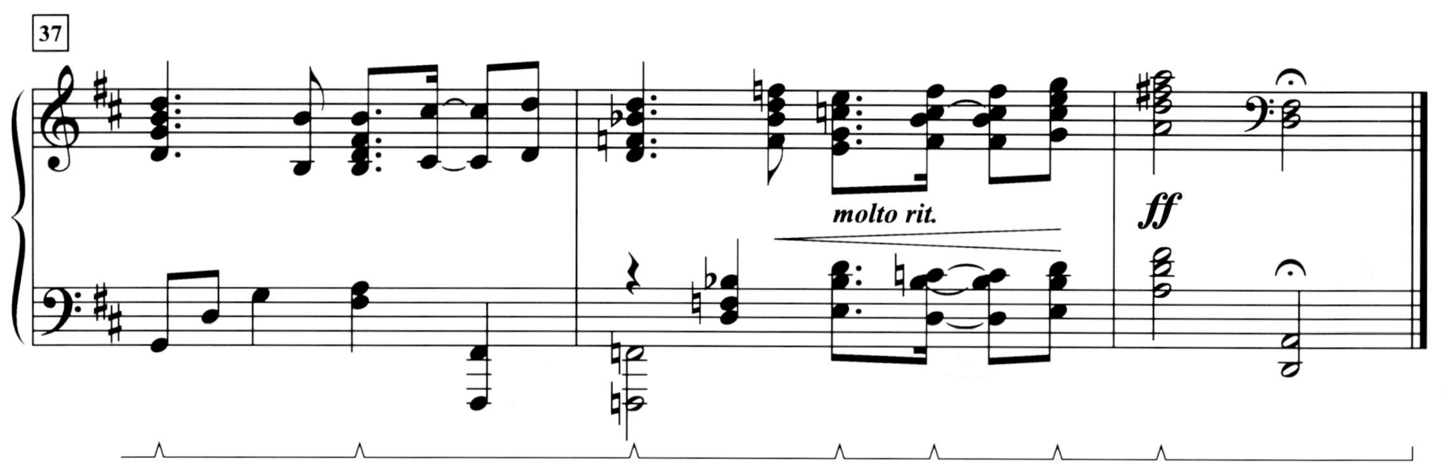

37
molto rit.
ff